What I Want Next...

30 Minutes to Reveal Your Future

Cathy Bonner

Sag Harbor Press: www.sagharborpress.org

ISBN: 0-9776602-0-6

Library of Congress Control Number: 2006900047

Submit all requests to: Cathy Bonner, P.O. Box 50381, Austin, TX, 78763 or cathy@whatiwantnext.com.

Layout by Terry Johnston

Text Editing by Sally Rice Jones

Some individuals names have been changed to protect their confidentiality or privacy.

What I Want Next *is the first*
in a series of books,
tapes, and training materials that can
transform your future.

It is dedicated to my friend,
Jane Hickie,
the genius behind the
What I Want Next Process.

Contents

Prologue . . . 1
Stories to Make You Strong . . . 5
The Power of the Process . . . 13
The Process and You . . . 19
The Choices We Make . . . 25
Changes Based On Reality . . . 31
Eyes On the Prize . . . 37
Getting "Unstuck" . . . 39
We Are Not Equally Motivated . . . 41
The ***What I Want Next*** Process . . . 45
Epilogue . . . 63
Ten More Copies of the Process . . . 65

Prologue

I had invited my parents to join us at our beach house for a shrimp boil during the Fourth of July weekend. At our Independence Day party, fifty pounds of shrimp and vegetables are cooked together in a huge pot on butane stove outside. We throw this seafood combination on tables covered with newspapers. Everyone dives in, selecting his or her favorite things to eat and dipping it all in melted butter.

I found myself getting irritated with my father during that visit because he was always complaining. He didn't feel well. Something was wrong. He couldn't stand or walk for very long.

I have always felt you had better be on your deathbed to constantly complain about how you feel. I have no patience for that. Isn't that just giving in to your negative thoughts?

And anyway, my father wasn't that old. He was just a few days away from turning seventy.

After my parents returned home, my father's doctor decided to operate on his back to relieve his chronic pain. Daddy was told the surgery would make walking and moving around easier.

Before the surgery, my father had lung x-rays to make sure he could handle the anesthesia. The whole family gathered in his hospital room to wait for him to be taken to the operating room.

Then the doctor walked in with Daddy's x-rays in his hand. The doctor's face was ashen. That is not something you want to see in the surgeon who is about to operate on you. "I am sorry," he said, unable to meet anyone's eyes. "We found something on your lung. A mass. This isn't good." He told us they could not operate that day. "We need to do more tests. We are 90% sure it is cancer."

I asked if he could remove it. The doctor shuffled and looked down at his feet. "No, it's too big," he said.

The next two days were a blur of CAT scans and biopsies. The full report after the first alarm was devastating...inoperable lung cancer, liver cancer, and cancer lesions on his brain.

Doctors came and went. Most of them said as little as possible, avoiding the hardest question. I finally cornered the oncologist and asked, "How long does he have?" The doctor said, "He could have as little as a month, or as much as six. But there won't be any recovery. He is dying."

What would you do if you were told you were living your last days? Not months, not years, but days. Would you travel the world and see what you never had time to see? Visit family and friends and tell them goodbye or the secrets they needed to know? Would you search for a miracle? Pray?

From the day my father was diagnosed with cancer, he only had thirty-two more days. He spent his time in chemotherapy and radiation treatments in a desperate effort to buy more time. None of us believed he would be gone so quickly. Our goodbyes could have been so much more direct. Our ability to communicate was never as strong as our love during that time. Time goes by so fast, particularly when denial is on the daily agenda.

What I Want Next asks you to imagine that you have little time left on earth. If you had a month to live, it would be a lot easier to know what you really wanted to do in your life, not what you think you should want to do.

So what do you want next in your life? In all likelihood, you have a great deal of time remaining. But hypothetically speaking, how would you live today if you knew you only had thirty-two tomorrows?

Stories to Make You Strong

Having been born in the middle of the twentieth century makes me one of the original baby boomers. As a boomer facing the second half of my life, I had settled into a comfortable and productive life that I loved.

We boomers think a lot about mortality. When a parent or someone close to you dies or when you have a health scare, you wake up to the idea that one day you, too, will take your last breath. The life you have lived will be over. That's what happened to me.

I have fair skin and light-colored eyes. I have exposed my body to years of sun. As I fried my skin in the search of the perfect tan, I can remember my mother saying, "You will be sorry one day."

Mom was right. I was more than sorry; I was terrified when my dermatologist informed me that I had a suspicious mole on my lower back. The growth was in a place I had never checked. It wasn't even in a spot that ever had sun damage. The doctor said it was probably benign, but he removed it and sent it to the lab for analysis.

The next week, when I went to have my stitches removed, the doctor told me the mole had been an early melanoma, the deadliest form of skin cancer. He would need to remove a bigger piece of tissue to make sure the cancer had not spread.

I was lucky. The cancer was *in situ*...meaning it had not spread.

Survivors will tell you that when they hear the word "cancer," they think the worst. While you wait for the treatment, and before you get the word that they got it all, you think about your mortality. I thought of it like this: I wasn't ready to leave the party. I kept thinking that I wasn't done yet. I certainly didn't want to go.

"The future ain't what it used to be."—Yogi Berra

It was during this time that my friend, Jane Hickie, gave me the ***What I Want Next*** Process to do for myself. I believe in the magic of synchronicity. The timing of this effort was no coincidence. I had come to an important crossroads in my life.

What an interesting thing to do—to think about what you want to have accomplished before the end of your life. The Process clarified my thoughts. It brought some things to the surface that I had unconsciously known about myself. I spent less than an hour distilling my thoughts. And my life turned in a new direction.

When I did my first ***What I Want Next*** Process, it took only thirty minutes to complete. After I finished, Jane, who developed the Process, met me for coffee to help interpret my results.

Jane Hickie and I have been friends for more than thirty years. We met through the work we shared in the early days of the women's movement. In the early 1970's, we banded together, working to start both the National Woman's Political Caucus and the Texas Women's Political Caucus. We burned with the injustices of the day. We scorched the institutions that held us back as well as the mossbacks that didn't believe in our cause—equality. Jane and I worked together for many causes and for many political candidates.

Together, with a small group of women consumed by the same fever, Jane and I helped start an educational, nonprofit organization called The Foundation for Women's Resources. We developed and operated programs and projects to improve women's lives in America.

We published books and produced a state women's history exhibit that was seen by over two million people. In the early 1980's, I led the Foundation and we developed leadership-training programs that still exist today as Leadership Texas, Leadership America, and PowerPipeline.

"Women are like snowflakes. One may melt, but working together, they can stop traffic."—Anonymous

---

During these thirty years of organizing women and helping them gain political power, many of our Foundation group went through life-changing experiences. We are a group of old friends that are more like family. We have gone through the "three D's" together: Death, Divorce, and Disaster.

In a way, this group of friends "raised" each other. We taught each other how to dress, speak in public, deal with the press, pass legislation, raise money, and even run for office. We went through so many life-changing stages together that when one of our group, Ann Richards, former Governor of Texas, wrote her autobiography, she thought about calling it, "Raising Kids...Raising Hell...Raisin Bran."

Jane Hickie developed the ***What I Want Next*** Process with input from some of the other Foundation members. For more than twenty years, Jane used the Process to define her own life and plan her career changes. She has shared the Process with many others who have used it to make decisions about their next moves, both personal and professional.

I believe in the power of stories. I will share the stories of people who have used the Process. I hope the stories help you see how you can create your future rather than allowing the future to be something that simply happens to you.

The future is not just a place where you will go. It is a place you can create.

When Jane insisted that I do the Process, I had a comfortable life. I owned a successful advertising agency. I had raised over $32 million and built the nation's first and only comprehensive women's history museum. I had two homes and lots of friends who helped me enjoy them.

I loved my life. I had financial security and a twenty-six-year relationship with a man who made me happy.

So I walked into the coffeehouse with my answers to the seven questions posed in the Process workbook. I told Jane I was overwhelmed by the ideas that the Process had stirred up about what I should do next in my life. Of course, I had approached the exercise with my Type A personality, and I now had lots of new assignments for things to be done by the end of that week.

Jane took one look at my Process answers and said, "Well, Cathy, this is pretty clear. You want to be a successful writer. It appears on your answers three times. You don't need to do nine new things.

You just need to pay attention to this common theme, and no matter what you do in the future, you need to write."

This is the beauty of the Process. It can strike you like a heat-seeking missile. It will help you recognize the burning desires hiding in the recesses of your mind and your heart.

What I Want Next is an easy-to-use tool that will help you learn what you truly want next in your life. Too many people go through life stuck in ruts. They go through the motions without considering whether they are doing those things that are truly important to them. These people live unconsciously.

"Don't mistake the edge of a rut for the horizon."
—James Patterson

What I Want Next is not just for people who are dying, stuck, or going through a life-changing crisis. You don't have to be facing the end of life, the end of a marriage, or the end of career to be in the right mind-set for evaluating your life. You just have to be a person who loves to discover new ideas and who is unafraid of taking inventory.

An old Arab proverb says, "When you go shopping for wisdom, be sure to visit every tent in the bazaar." There are lots of "tents" in this book. Some of them contain peer wisdom. Some offer expert wisdom. Some reveal wisdom hidden in plain sight.

For example, during a family trip to Alaska, we took a helicopter ride to the top of a glacier and rode briefly on a dogsled. I say briefly, because those little dogs (each one only weighs about 25 pounds) can't pull too many fat Americans for very long.

Back on our cruise ship, we heard a woman named Libby Riddles speak. In 1985, Libby was the first woman to win the Iditarod, the grueling 1,100-mile Alaska, dogsled race that starts in Anchorage and ends in Nome.

The Iditarod is a treacherous race. It lasts for three weeks. It's just you and your dogs out in the Alaska wilderness in double-digit subzero weather. You feed your dogs first, just as, in an airplane, you'd put your own oxygen mask on first before helping others, because the dogs are your ticket out of a sea of snow.

I asked Libby how she became tough enough to finish the race. When she moved to Alaska as a young woman, the first thing she did was to go around and talk to all the old "mushers," those men who had finished or won the race in past years. She spent hours listening to their stories of success and failure.

Libby told us, "Half of getting tough is just knowing all the stories."

"Half of getting tough is just knowing all the stories."
—Libby Riddles

In this book, there are stories of discovery. They are stories of change and renewal. You will see, in the stories, that just like a heat-seeking missile, you sometimes have to make mid-course corrections on your way to your target

One day, Jane went to her hairdresser in a rather distraught state. "I just hate my hair," she said. Her hairdresser replied, "Then change your mind."

What you think you are, you will be. If you want to change your life, you must first change your mind.

With the help of a practicing clinical psychologist, Dr. Melinda Longtain, this book will help you understand the ways in which people can and do change their lives. We will tell you the stories of how the Process has helped people evolve and the different ways people become "unstuck."

There used to be a moving company with the slogan "If we can get it loose, we can move it." The first part of this work involves loosening up your mind. The second part then becomes actually changing your mind.

"If we can get it loose. we can move it."
—Moving company slogan

Changing your mind is the hardest work you will ever do. You can't simply follow someone else's beaten path. Too often, the beaten path is full of beaten people!

You can use this Process repeatedly throughout your life. Keep in mind that you cannot change everything about your life at once. Very likely, you will feel the need to take a hard look at different areas of your life at different stages. One year, it may be your career. Another time, it might be relationships or your spiritual life. Extra copies are provided so you may do the Process again and again at various junctures in your life.

"It's like driving a car at night.
You never see further than your headlights,
but you can make the whole trip that way."
—E. L. Doctorow

The Power of the Process

Most of the women in our Foundation have remade their lives several times over. One woman started out as a secretary and is now a Federal Magistrate. One started life as an unwed teenage mother and has recently retired from the judge's bench. One college dean started climbing mountains and took on both Mount Kilimanjaro and Mount Everest. One young lawyer's first case was an uncontested divorce. Her second case, argued before the United States Supreme Court, was historic. She won *Roe v. Wade*. Another raised four children, taught school, and ended up the Governor of Texas.

My friend, Jane Hickie, has been part of this Foundation since its beginning. She is a successful lawyer, lobbyist, and business consultant. She has survived financial disaster, managed political campaigns, and made and lost fortunes, reinventing herself many times over the last thirty years.

Jane created this Process in response to her life's challenges and quandaries at each of its many junctures. She has revised it many times to make it better and more relevant.

In early 1980s, Jane was finishing law school and working at the Travis County Courthouse. The courthouse sits between the heart of downtown Austin, Texas, and the State Capitol. It used to have a jail on its top floor. The rest of the courthouse is filled with elected officials who torment each other.

At the time when Jane worked there, the jail nurse was a defrocked doctor who believed in the mystical power of the color blue and who served drugs to the inmates on a "come and get it" basis. Jane recounts that one day she went searching for storage space in a coat closet next to the county judge's office. There, she discovered that the medical examiner had hidden body parts in canning jars—with the former owners' names pasted on the lids.

Another public official, the county clerk, was obsessing about the pigeons that regularly fouled her car from their perch above the parking lot. Having heard that pigeons are deathly afraid of snakes, she sent the janitor to buy $54 worth of rubber snakes. However, the only ledges the janitor could reach were outside the jail at the top of the building, where the holding cells were located. As a result, the barely sobered teenagers jailed the night before woke up to see "flying" snakes.

It was pretty clear to Jane that she had to get out of there. But where to go and what to do? Jane didn't have a clue, so she went to one of our Foundation friends and asked whether she had any ideas on figuring out what to do next.

Jane's friend told her to imagine everything she wanted to do in her life. Next, she should focus on what she would actually spend an hour doing in the next week to advance her toward her goals. If she couldn't find an hour to work on a goal, she should consider it no more than a fantasy and strike it off her list.

Jane pulled out an enormous newsprint pad and three colored pens, and set out to imagine a new life. There were no limits on her wants—she was then only 32 years old. She felt she could do, or be, anything.

Jane wrote that she wanted to have a loving family, travel widely, raise dogs, be a spy, get healthy and stay healthy, be a good daughter, make a lot of money, give away a lot of money, enjoy her friends, be a respected political leader, make a difference for women, and live with great art.

"When the gods wish to punish us, they answer our prayers."— Oscar Wilde

Short of spying, Jane succeeded in meeting all her goals because of the Process, but the road to her success was indirect.

Working this Process correctly will mean looking the facts squarely in the face. For example, every time Jane worked the Process, it showed her that she wanted a healthy life. "Get healthy" showed up on every list she made. The hitch was that she didn't stop drinking, even though she knew better.

By now, it was 1988, and Jane appeared fairly jaunty at the time. But inside, she felt as though she had been "vacuumed." She used exciting and hilarious behavior to distract herself from the truth about her life.

I remember one wild weekend in New York when we all went to celebrate a friend's birthday. A group of us stayed up for 24 hours. We even tried to rent a helicopter to fly to Atlantic City so we could make a killing rolling the dice. I thank God that none of us had a credit card that would allow us to rent a helicopter. On the way home, we gave the poor flight attendants fits with our antics.

But of course, the party had to stop. One night, flying into Washington, D.C., Jane realized that she didn't care whether or not the plane landed safely. She was stunned to realize how little it mattered to her whether she lived or died.

Jane didn't look bad. In fact, the photographs from that time show someone who was thin, and therefore apparently fit. But she recalls that her stomach hurt all the time.

Each morning, Jane would decide not to drink any alcohol. But then someone would call, or friends would drop by. Drinks and dinner would result. She rarely felt drunk. In fact (and this is worse), she "didn't feel anything."

It took time before Jane's life became painful enough to force her to sit down and work the Process. What did she want next? How ridiculous, she thought. She didn't care enough to want anything at all.

Finally, as she stared at the paper, pencil, and a timer, she tried to imagine what she wanted to do in her life. As her timer ticked away, some important thoughts emerged: Jane wanted to feel content, be a runner, hike, live to a very old age, be strong, and never again be embarrassed by her own behavior. She wanted to stop the stomachaches and never spend another evening with people who were drunk and boring.

Her next step was to select the three most important things on her list. She picked "to get healthy," "to not be embarrassed," and "to like herself," since those choices seemed to represent her core values. However, picking three broad statements also made it easier to fudge on the practical steps she needed to take during the following week.

It was a struggle for Jane to name the specific tasks that would help her feel better. At first, she tried writing that she would go to a gym, talk with a friend who had quit drinking, and read more about alcoholism. Erasing those halfhearted, halfway ideas, she stared at her calendar for the coming week and then at her list of desires. Finally, she confronted the painful commitment she had to make. With regret, she decided that she must enroll in an alcoholic counseling program that required attendance every night for a month.

"Courage is the price that life extracts for granting peace."
—Amelia Earhart

It was what Jane really wanted and needed next, and it worked.

Years later, Jane realized she next needed to face financial reality. Serving on the staff of Governor Ann Richards had led to an interesting job in Washington. However, four years as a public employee with Washington expenses was no strategy for financial well-being.

She worked the Process once more, focusing on ideas for increasing her income. At that juncture, she couldn't justify hobbies, travel, good works, pets, or losing five pounds. She had to concentrate on her financial needs for her family's sake.

Jane was a lobbyist with experience in both Washington and Texas, and she had powerful friends in both places. Working the Process made it clear that what she wanted next was to join a Washington law firm with ties to Texas. After a focused networking effort, she found the right opportunity. The law firm partnership was a perfect fit for six years.

Several times since then, Jane has revisited the Process. Most recently, she was amazed to uncover a new focus on a search for some spiritual connection. Suddenly Jane, the life of the party, the extrovert's extrovert, was looking into books on spirituality. She read and listened to books on meditation. However, every time she attempted to meditate in a traditional way, she fell asleep.

It happened at this time that Jane's father died. His great joy in life had been golf. As a distraction one day, just to get out of the house, Jane went to the golf course. Somehow she felt closer to her father there. Although she played terribly, there were moments when she connected with the ball in a way that seemed effortless. In these moments, Jane sensed the state of peace and inner calm described in the meditation books she had read.

Later, on a whim, she signed up for a watercolor class at a local art museum. Once again, Jane found that, as she concentrated on her fledgling efforts to paint, she lost consciousness of the teacher, the other students, and even the inadequacy of her own attempts at art. Again, she was experiencing a different state and its accompanying inner peace.

Today, Jane lives in Seattle, where she has opened a new office for Public Strategies, an international business strategy firm. She marvels that the simple pleasures of golf and painting satisfy her need for a spiritual connection.

The Process enabled Jane to feel her way to a new dimension and to find it in the ways that suited her best. What began as a mysterious, difficult process later yielded some fairly basic solutions. The "surprises," as it turned out, were hidden in plain sight.

"Yesterday is history. Tomorrow is a mystery.
Today is a gift. That is why we call it 'the present.'"
—Anonymous

The Process and You

Before you spend the next thirty minutes completing the Process, we need to be crystal clear about what the Process will not do for you:

- It is not a formula for making you a millionaire.
- It is not thirty minutes in your life intended to stir up inner conflict or make you give up on important relationships.
- It is not a half-hour catharsis or crystal ball for locating your missing spiritual guide, leader, angel, or compass.

What I Want Next is a method of finding the true answer to this question, "What I want next is ________________." You will fill in the blank at the end of thirty minutes of structured brainstorming.

Notice the word "true." This is very important. Most people lie to themselves all the time. These lies often fall under the category of "safe harbors." You're never hurt by your lie. It doesn't sink you. It just stalls you out.

The lie is usually about what you want in your future. But, what will make you truly happy? What are you missing? What new accomplishment or adventure will make your heart sing?

This method will help you dig down deep to get the real answer. If you are wise, you will act on it. The answer will be true when it comes from your heart, as well as your head.

This method will help you move out of that safe harbor known as the status quo into the deeper waters of success and failure. I have always learned more from my failures than my successes.

This Process does not require rebirthing, time on a therapist's couch, or a primal scream. It does provide a very crisp awareness of who you really are, how you really function, and what it will take for you to make new things happen in your life.

It will help you see your core values. Your core values are the most important things you own. They are the values that all your choices and behaviors are based upon. If you are not true and honest to these core values, nothing in your life will work properly.

Let's say you've bought new tires for your car. The warranty says they are good for 60,000 miles. But if they are not aligned properly, you will only get 25,000 miles from them before they wear out.

"Your values are the tires upon which you ride, so your life had better be aligned with them if you want maximum performance."
—Dr. Melinda Longtain

So what are your core values?

One woman, Michele, first used the ***What I Want Next*** Process in the spring of 2003. At that point in her life, she had been at the same company for more than twelve years. Having had the good fortune to join Dell Computer Corporation (now Dell, Inc.) in 1991, Michele was part of the extended team who built it from the small company of those early, entrepreneurial days into today's global technology marketing force.

Although the company's future was very promising, the excitement that comes with being part of a growing and dynamic company changes as the company matures. While she still enjoyed working with most of her colleagues, Michele felt a longing for something different, something that would present new challenges.

Using the ***What I Want Next*** Process for the first time, Michele discovered that she wanted to do the things that one would do on a vacation. She wanted to exercise, learn about wine and food, and visit all the continents and great cities of the world. She also looked beyond this immediate vacation time and discovered that she wanted to teach and write, to enjoy time with those important to her—and to drive a fast car. Armed with those discoveries, she bought a new bicycle, bought a fast sedan, and spent several weeks in France tasting wine, eating well, and enjoying life.

Her time at Dell had given her a financial freedom that, surprisingly, made her choices all the more difficult. Should she start a business, go back to school, or take a trip around the world? Should she run a nonprofit dedicated to a cause she cared about? So many options were available to her, yet none excited her.

So, Michele tried the ***What I Want Next*** Process another time. The new results told her that she still had the drive to learn and work. It helped that she had put into action what she had learned from her first use of the Process. From those lessons, she knew that she enjoyed eating well much more than she would ever enjoy cooking well. And while she enjoyed travel, it would be no more than an occasional pastime. Although her intended focus was professional, the results also reinforced how important her personal life was to her. Spending time with those who mattered most was the core value that allowed her to take the next step. She decided to build on her eighteen years of high technology experience.

The intellectual challenge that comes from working on cutting-edge legal and policy issues was exciting to her. She decided to be open to pursuing this work, even though, technically, she never would have to work again. The results were not a surprise to her. The gift of the ***What I Want Next*** Process is that it allows you, as Michele says, "to have a candid conversation with yourself about what it is you do, in fact, really want."

About the same time, Michele was aggressively recruited for a new job at one of the premier technology companies in the country. She took the job and the new challenge. Funny how the universe works once you get clear about your core values and what you really want.

An authentic life is one in which you craft a career that reflects your own core values. But if a career is not part of your future, it is still important to know and use your core values when you are deciding what to do next.

When my sister, Lisa, did the Process, she was a stay-at-home mother of five. Before she started the Process, she felt like she should desire a career or new job. After the Process, she felt so relieved to know that what she really wanted next was to help her children through their own personal and health issues. She wanted to spend her time ensuring that her family was on the road to a better future.

"Finally," she said, "I can see in black and white that I don't need to feel guilty about not pursuing a career outside the home. Helping my children through these rough times is what I really want to do."

It was very affirming to Lisa that she could give up a superimposed model of what the world was saying to her and stay on track with her family. Her common theme was the importance of protecting her family. Sometimes making no change is the right thing to do next.

I hope you will use the Process to find the next steps in your life—steps that will be in keeping with your core values. If you find them, you will probably agree with my favorite philosopher, Mae West, who said, "Too much of a good thing is...wonderful."

"The future belongs to those who believe in the beauty of their dreams."
—Eleanor Roosevelt

The Choices We Make

On election night, November 1994, my boss and friend Ann Richards, then Governor of Texas, was up for re-election against George W. Bush. It was still early in the evening, but all day long the exit-poll results coming in from the field had not been good.

When Ann was elected in 1990, I sold my advertising agency and joined her cabinet as executive director of the Texas Department of Commerce. I had the best job in the state government because I got to put together "deals" bringing new business and industry to Texas. I left government in 1994 to work on Ann's re-election campaign.

About two weeks before the election, I knew Ann would probably lose. I was traveling with her a lot during the last days of the campaign, and something felt wrong. The crowds were not as big, nor as enthusiastic, as they had been during the 1990 campaign.

I believe that people never had a clear picture as to why Ann wanted to be re-elected, or of what she would do for them. Politics is all "image," and the second time around, Ann's image as a "new type of leader" was not carrying the day. George W. Bush looked like the new type of leader, and he was saying all the things the polls said people wanted to hear.

Governor Richards came to the campaign headquarters shortly after the polls closed at 7:00 p.m. Early returns trickled in, and by 9:00 p.m. the trend was clear: Ann was going to lose the first election she had ever lost in her political career.

I remember that Ann seemed so composed and matter-of-fact. Some of her children became upset and started to cry. By 10:00 p.m., Ann was standing in front of thousands of deflated supporters and campaign workers, telling them, "This is not the end of the world. Just the end of a campaign."

Ann recalls that she may have grieved for all of twenty miniutes over this loss. The truth is, she felt energized by the opportunity of a new life even though she had no idea where she would live or work after moving out of the Governor's Mansion. She knew that whatever happened next would be a great new adventure.

In planning her next steps, one of the first things Ann did, with Jane's help, was to define her core values. Being two people unafraid to break new ground or old rules, they drew up a list of criteria that Ann would use for determining any future steps.

The list was predicated on Ann's lifelong belief that a person should always say yes to any new opportunity, unless it is illegal, could harm you, or could hurt others. As Ann likes to say, "The correct answer is always YES." Here are the values Ann decided to use in whatever came next in her life:

1. I want to work with people I like.
2. I want to work and get paid for it.
3. I want to travel for fun, not just for business.
4. I want to learn new things.
5. I want to leave the world a better place for my having been in it.

Today, Ann Richards works for a company and with people she likes and respects. Her financial future is secure. As she puts it, she won't have to live out her old age in a trailer parked in one of her kid's driveways.

She works hard to elect the kind of people she feels will make the world a better place. She has traveled to every state in the nation and every continent except Australia (where she will go soon) and she still learns along the way.

In the second half of her life, she uses these criteria to decide where she goes, what she does, and what she works on. In the face of many choices and demands upon her time, this process of elimination allows her to prioritize more easily.

"Seize the moment. Remember all those women on the* Titanic *who waved off the dessert cart."
—Erma Bombeck

The Process helps you see that some things are worth doing because they move you toward your goals, while other things do not. Focusing on your goals allows you to live in a more positive way than you do when you are caught in a trap of acting unconsciously.

Think of it like playing basketball or football. You can play the first half any way you want. When you are young, you can "waste" time experimenting with ideas, moves, and attitudes because you are just testing the waters. But how will you play the second half? After all, it's your last chance.

Will you play with wild abandon, just like you did when you drove the bumper cars at the fair? Will you bounce around, going in no particular direction, except the one you are pushed into? Or will you play with dignity and determination, after taking time to make plans based on truth and reality?

There is little time to waste. In the second half, you must focus. Will you play the rest of the game with purpose and vision? Or will you repeat the strategies you used in the first half and simply hope for a better outcome?

I met a man I will call Henderson (not his real name) who did the Process as part of a corporate team-building exercise. I had never seen him before, and have not seen him since that time.

Before the thirty minutes had lapsed, Henderson jumped out of his seat, picked up the Process workbook, and left the room. He looked agitated and distracted. Everyone else was still completing their Process workbooks, and didn't seem to notice. I certainly did. I made a mental note to follow up later and see what had caused such a drastic reaction.

The next day, I tracked Henderson down at his office number. He answered, but said he would have to call me back later.

I was surprised when he called me at home later that night. Although hesitant, he seemed eager to talk about his reaction to the Process. I mainly listened, because I had few skills to use in response to what he was telling me.

Henderson said the Process had made a profound impact on him. He said he was living a double life. To the outside world, he was a typical electronic engineer with a wife and two kids in suburbia. But secretly, he was having an affair with a woman who worked for a foreign government whom he had met on a business trip to Russia. They had met years ago during the days of Perestroika, the first opening of Communist Russia to the outside world in the 1980's.

He didn't say for sure, but I took this to mean that the woman was, or had been, connected to the Soviet government. It sounded like she had ultimately moved to the States or at least traveled here often, because they had been seeing each other on a regular basis for years.

Henderson was distraught because the Process showed him that the common theme of his life was based on lies. The lies he had told and the lie he was living. His children were grown. His relationship with his wife had degenerated into a comfortable, "best friends" relationship, but he knew she would leave him if he told her the truth. What he wanted next was to stop the affair and live an authentic life without losing his wife and his family.

Now here was a guy who was about to make a big course correction. Cataclysmic change was required here.

I was amazed that Henderson was telling me this story. He seemed desperate to tell someone what the Process had done for him. I was sympathetic about the hard work that lay ahead for him. I told him clarity is the best we can hope for in living an authentic life, and I wished him well.

Usually the Process brings changes that are not as dramatic as Henderson's. We see with our own brand of clarity that smaller changes can really make a difference in living a better life. But where and how do we start to change?

Changes Based On Reality

Keep in mind that you've got just twenty-four hours a day. You must be realistic. If you add something new to your schedule, you must let something else go. Give yourself the freedom to take less-meaningful actions off your calendar to make room for the changes based on reality.

If you already feel overburdened with tasks, you need to weed out activities that no longer have meaning or value for you—or, at least, not enough to warrant the time and effort required.

Periodic sorting and culling keeps our closets free of unnecessary clutter. We need to do the same for our lives. If spending time with certain people in your social circle does not help you meet your goals, or even keeps you from meeting your goals, let them go or limit your exposure to them. If you serve on committees, have volunteer assignments, or have taken on too much at work, it may be time to review the whole picture and redefine the boundaries on your current commitments.

Don't worry or wonder about what someone else would consider worthy goals—or worthy first steps. Comparing yourself to others will only confuse you and get you thinking about the one thing you cannot change or do anything about—someone else's opinion.

"If you want to conduct an orchestra,
you must turn your back on the crowd."
—Anonymous

Dr. Longtain once had a client with some unrealistic ideas about what he wanted next. One of his supposedly smaller goals included arriving at work by 8:00 a.m. every day so he could get more accomplished. As he was self-employed, there was no real consequence for his arriving to work later than that.

The only problem was that he just could not do it. He was forever setting the alarm for 6:30 and ignoring it until 8:30. Once he got up, he would beat himself up for being unsuccessful at something as simple as getting out of bed.

She told him to take early rising off his list—he was clearly not a morning person. Since his life does not require that he begin work early, he should revel in that freedom. Things have been much easier since he did so. He no longer starts his day defining himself as a loser.

This is a Process where the answers will be unique to you. One size is not supposed to fit all. In fact, there is no such thing as one size. Remember that even appliances, hats, and cars come in all sizes. It is important to find the size you need for your situation.

If your goal is to write a book, then expecting to write a chapter during the very first week is probably overly optimistic. Writing a book is a marathon, and people train for marathons by running short distances in the beginning. Try to set reasonable and appropriate markers for your progress towards your overall goal.

Even Lance Armstrong had to figure out how to win the Tour de France.

Lance started his Lance Armstrong Foundation to educate people about testicular cancer and to lead the way in cancer research and survivorship issues. He was a cancer survivor at this time, but he had not yet won the Tour de France. He had raced in the Tour several times, but never won the event.

Despite his rigorous training regimen and his almost superhuman lung capacity, he couldn't win the Tour until he learned how to win it. He put together the knowledge and science that allowed him to develop a winning strategy.

Lance's commitment to a strict training strategy is legendary. When he is in training, he weighs every ounce of food and drink that goes into his body. Lance didn't win his first Tour race until he devised the plan on how to ride with his team strategically.

His strategy includes pacing himself and his team for peak performance. He learned not to charge on the bike just because his competitors were charging. He stuck to his game plan on his timetable, and it put him on the winner's podium in Paris a record seven times.

It doesn't matter how fast you start the race if you cannot finish. And the only person in this particular race is you.

At the end of the year 2000, many top-level officials of the Clinton administration were preparing for new lives. Soon there would be a new president. New people would fill thousands of jobs in the new administration.

During this time, some of these people asked former Governor Ann Richards for her help. They viewed her as someone who had successfully negotiated the transition from public service to private prosperity. With speeches, the law firm, television punditry, Democratic Party fundraising, and travel with friends and family, Ann had created the life that these people wanted.

Ann's advice was to use the ***What I Want Next*** Process to figure out what they wanted to do next. Ann would bring Jane to their offices to do the Process with them. Soon Ann and Jane were touring a series of government agencies, meeting with senior public officials who were hesitant (but curious) about trying this or any other process.

These high-ranking public officials listened to Ann's introduction and Jane's description of the Process and its results. Eyebrow arched, one said in a clipped tone, "Actually, I'm afraid to find out what I want next." Ann and Jane were stunned.

Some people are afraid to find out what they really want. In some cases, people simply complain about lousy relationships rather than planning steps to improve their situations. They obsess over the misery of their traps: "My husband is overbearing, controlling." "There's no sex." "She/he hates my pets." "She/he won't travel." "She/he is jealous, boring, overweight, neurotic, unwilling to change." So is this what you want?

Others didn't seem to want to reflect at all. Some were locked in a frenzy of activity in an exhausting effort at avoiding themselves. Perhaps they didn't think they deserved to have what they wanted. Some believed that life is hard, and then you die. Period.

One person even told Jane that she didn't want to try the Process because she wanted to be thin and rich, and she knew neither goal was possible. A goal like this certainly is impossible if that is what you believe. Stop driving with one foot on the gas and the other foot on the brake.

"I miss 100% of the shots I never take."
—Wayne Gretskzy

We enjoy privilege in our lives. We have an obligation to understand our gifts and put them to good use.

"An unexamined life is not worth living."—Socrates

One person in Washington, D.C., was not afraid to find out what the Process could do for her: Jane Holmes Dixon, the second in command at the Episcopal Diocese.

Each Episcopal church is required to welcome the bishop of its diocese for a visit. But in Bishop Dixon's case, some priests actually refused to welcome her. They vacated their churches to avoid greeting a female bishop.

Bishop Dixon speaks with a Southern accent and radiates generosity of spirit. She is short, substantial, and awe-inspiring in her robes and with her staff. Jane had met Bishop Dixon during one of her church visits, but was surprised to get a call from her asking if she would meet with her to talk about the Process.

After years of putting up with discrimination, Bishop Dixon was ready to quit her post. After Jane outlined the Process to her, the bishop took it home and promptly completed it. It seemed simple enough and was easy to do. At the end, it became clear to her that what she wanted to do next was to take a leave of absence and visit the Middle East. So she got up her nerve to say that she needed a break.

Much to her surprise, her boss told her that he was going to retire—and he wanted Bishop Dixon to take over his spot at the top. She said she would consider the offer, but needed at least six months off to recharge her batteries. Because her boss felt so sure she was the right person, he offered to delay his retirement until she returned.

So Bishop Dixon went on a much-deserved sabbatical. She and her husband took what she calls "the trip of a lifetime" to Egypt and the Holy Land.

When Bishop Dixon returned to the United States, she revisited the Process and decided to stay on at the diocese. She then became the second woman in America to be named a head bishop—and one of just three in the entire world.

The next time Jane saw Bishop Dixon was on television in 2001. After the September 11 terrorist attacks when the nation was comforted by the service at National Cathedral, Bishop Jane Holmes Dixon presided at our country's service of mourning.

Looking back, Bishop Dixon says she would never have seen her need for a break in her career if she had not done the Process. Had she not discovered she could make realistic changes, she probably would have stayed at her job, gotten burned out, and eventually would have left. Instead, she was able to remain in a life of service, on her own terms. The bishop is retired from the clergy now, but continues to use the Process in the classes she teaches for senior citizens.

Eyes on the Prize

You should see this opportunity with new eyes. You are entitled to make the best choices you can for yourself. These choices are our only real entitlements in life. They lead us down paths that lead to still more choices, and further to more paths and choices.

In her psychology practice, Dr. Melinda Longtain helps people who often cannot see what their choices are, who are angered by the choices facing them, or who want guarantees as to where their choices will lead them.

Remember that when we stop seeing our choices, we are no longer in charge of our lives. At this point, we have become "effects," not causes. Our loss of personal empowerment and initiative will cost us our self-respect, personal dignity, and our well-being.

Renee was a broadcaster who had left her professional life behind ten years before. She had given up a career that had brought her acknowledgement and acclaim. She did so because her two children needed her. The kids were floundering in adolescence. Either Renee or her executive husband needed to be at home on a 24/7 basis to keep these children out of harm's way.

Renee and her husband talked it over and decided that she would make the move home because, even though she had risen up the journalistic chain, she had hit the "glass ceiling." It didn't look like her career could go much further. Her husband's career was on a projected CEO track. His chances seemed much more promising.

Now the kids were in college and Renee was feeling confused and frustrated. Should she go back to work? Should she start over in a new profession? Would anyone want to hire a 55-year-old journalist who had been out of the workplace for the last ten years? Renee was in a woman's group that did the Process. She spoke up when I asked about feedback from the Process.

"I found out something very interesting," she said. "I came up with this final sentence: What I want next is to build a place, a home or retreat, that nonprofit groups can use to raise money. I know a lot about organizing households. I want to put that to use for the betterment of my world."

I asked Renee what the common theme was that led her to this discovery. She had finally realized that the second half of her life was going to be about "giving back" to the next generation. It was not going to be about trying to recreate a career in an industry she had no respect for anymore. "I am thrilled to finally put a voice to my desire," she said.

Getting "Unstuck"

The Process gives you a chance to change your mind, or at least to think about your future in a different way. Dr. Steven Tomlinson was a professor of economics at a major university. He says, "If growing up doesn't make you wiser, it is not worth it."

He became a fan of the Process because, as he puts it, it helps you see the relationship between your soul and your will. This is a hard concept for most people to grasp. For Steven, if you can figure out the answer (or answers) to this last step, you can be the person you were meant to be. As he puts it, "unraveling this puzzle makes life truly worth living."

For example, when Steven was an assistant professor, he was very torn between three major, competing personal goals—to get tenure, become a playwright, or become a minister. Tenure was not a likely possibility if he continued the status quo. Or, he wondered, should he jump into the deep end and develop his theatrical writing and acting talents? These, he valued because he was passionate about helping people face their emotions and challenge their thinking.

Steven also was passionate about theology and ethics. Increasingly, he found himself integrating his ideas on spirituality into both his teaching and his playwriting. Should he bear down and get serious about his academic career? Move to New York and become a playwright? Enter the ministry? A more diverse set of quandaries would be hard to imagine, but Steven eventually did work through it.

Seeking advice and a pair of fresh ears, Steven took his quest to his priest. His priest said it was stupid—yes stupid—to approach life as if it were a checklist. We are not supposed to check off career decisions or life options one at a time and then move on to the next. Steven's priest told him that he shouldn't sacrifice any of these things—because they were all things he genuinely loved. He advised Steven to find a way to keep all three of his energies active in his life. Otherwise, he said, "You won't be the person you are supposed to be."

When Steven did his Process, the goals he listed in Step 3 were to (1) write a play, (2) lead a workshop, (3) spend time with his best friends, and (4) take walks with his mate. In the end, he boiled all of his desires down to one major goal that actually surprised him. Out of the blue, he came up with an idea to lead a retreat about money and the soul, where he could hear the thoughts of his best and wisest friends.

In his teaching, Steven needed to be able to talk about the spiritual side of accumulating wealth, as well as the ethical side of business decisions. In addition, he would also need to fulfill his need to be creative, to perform, and to convey his wisdom through his wit and verbal abilities.

Today, Steven is an accomplished performing artist who entertains audiences with his plays about ethics, politics, and morality. The *Austin Chronicle* named Steven "Austin's Best Monologist." He wrote and performs his one-man play called "American Fiesta."

"The Process points you toward your next step by making a promise with you instead of a threat. It shrinks the horizon down to nothing."
— Dr. Steven Tomlinson

We Are Not Equally Motivated

Now it is time to discuss another critical topic: motivation. How do you get motivated to work toward your goals?

There is a truth in life that most books on motivation do not mention. It's a truth that most of us are afraid to admit. Perhaps it's politically incorrect.

The secret truth is that we are not created equal.

For example, some people's metabolisms let them eat anything they want without gaining weight. Some are born with flawless skin that requires nothing more than soap at night. Some are born to make good grades without having to study.

So it is with this thing called motivation. Actually, "motivation" is an overused word that encompasses a broad spectrum of behaviors. Motivation is being capable of the effort and focus necessary to accomplish a goal. That collapses into one very simple thing—self-discipline.

The hallmark of self-discipline is the capacity for delayed gratification. Sound pretty boring? Is it too serious to consider? This is important, because it signals another way in which we are not created equal.

Researchers have put candy in a room and left children alone in the room with instructions to not eat the candy. They promise the children they can eat the candy later. Guess what? Some of the kids can leave the candy alone. Some simply cannot.

Dr. Melinda Longtain's adolescent daughter, Riley, was born with an uncanny ability to delay gratification. She demonstrated it at a medical checkup when she was just six years old.

Riley approached her checkup with great calm. The preceding year, she had questioned her pediatrician at length as to whether she would get a shot the next time. She is the type of child who actually has a panic attack when it is time for a shot and has to be held down. The doctor had promised Riley that it would be a non-shot year. Riley left the office in relief, knowing that she had a two-year reprieve. You know where this story is going, right?

Riley went for her six-year checkup with a cool head, because a promise had been made. Near the end of the exam, she reminded the doctor of that promise. The doctor took a deep breath and informed Riley that she would, in fact, need a booster shot.

Riley was given the choice to get the shot then and there, or to return for it later in the summer. When Melinda's daughter, at age six, made the difficult choice to get the shot over with, she was making a unique choice that her parents did not train her to make. That self-discipline was in her genetic makeup.

This is the same child who chooses to get her homework and chores out of the way before the weekend begins, putting the fun things on hold. Yet she dearly loves to have fun.

A person's ability to make choices based on delayed gratification is there when he or she is born. So, what looks like self-discipline and sacrifice is really an innate ability to inhibit the desire to feel good at the moment.

"Self-discipline is the willingness to experience something hard, difficult, or uncomfortable because we have decided we must, we are supposed to, or we just want to."
—Dr. Melinda Longtain

So what does a child's compliance have to do with you? Were you blessed with that ability to subordinate your impulse for fun and easy times to take on whatever challenges or goals you face? If so, this whole process of acting on your decision about what to do next is going to be easy for you. In fact, you have probably already used this quality with a fair amount of success.

Or perhaps you are in the same club as I am, the "Mañana Club." If so, it is time to give yourself a break. Forgive yourself for previous attempts to make major changes that did not work. Do not hold yourself hostage for past failures. Stop comparing yourself to others who seem to be masters of self-discipline.

It's not a natural feeling when you are fighting your own DNA.

"You really have to love yourself to get anything done in this world."
—Lucille Ball

It is important to understand that setbacks need not be thought of as out-and-out failures. The fact that it is more difficult for you to change does not need to cause you shame. Rather it means that the path toward your goal may not be straight. Jane's certainly wasn't. She had to fight some inner demons. Your path toward your goals may wander from time to time. But when you finally accomplish your goals, consider yourself an overachiever, because you had to go against your inborn nature to get there. One of America's finest poets wrote about it in this way:

"Something we were withholding made us weak until we found it was ourselves."
—Robert Frost

The What I Want Next Process

Before you do your first Process, you need to assemble your tools:

- A watch with a second hand, or some kind of timer.
- A pencil.
- Your calendar for the next week.

Next, take a look at what a completed Process looks like. I show you my own example of a Process here to demonstrate how you build toward the final step of deciding what you want next. I hope you can see from this example that common themes develop. Also, notice how you use your core values to eliminate options and zero in on that final sentence to incorporate several of your most important needs.

Remember, the Process is designed to be completed in just 30 minutes, and there are no wrong answers.

Example of a Completed Process

Step 1

Spend three minutes listing items to answer this question:

"By the end of my life, what do
I want to have done?"

- Write a book
- Spend my summers learning at Chautauqua
- Produce a movie
- Learn to paint
- Win the Nobel Peace Prize
- Add an academic degree
- Make the Women's Museum a catalyst for improving women's lives
- Visit every continent
- Live and study abroad
- Help elect a woman president

There are no limits…no boundaries…the list should include whatever comes to mind…personal or professional…as large or small as you imagine.

Step 2

Spend three minutes listing items to answer this question:

"By one year from today,
what do I want to have done?"
A year from now is: January 5, 2005 (date)

- To have written a book
- To have transitioned into a new career or revenue-producing life to secure my financial future
- To have secured a sustaining endowment for the Women's Museum
- To have taken my entire family on a family vacation/reunion

Step 3

Spend three minutes listing items to answer this question:

"I just found out I have thirty days to live. What do I want to have done in these thirty days?"

- Write a book to leave behind that shares my heart and mind
- Set up financial trusts for my loved ones
- Have a going-away party with my friends and family
- Visit Chautauqua, the beach, Broadway, and old friends
- Play lots of golf
- Write a screenplay
- Write some poems

Step 4

Look back at each of the first three steps. Circle the three items on each list that are most important to you. Then, copy them into the grid.

Note: Items may appear more than once in this grid.

Step 1	Step 2	Step 3
Write a book	To have written a book	Write a book
Make museum a catalyst for improving women's lives	To have transitioned into a new money-making career	Set up financial trusts
Spend summers learning in Chautauqua	To have secured a sustaining endowment for the museum	Have a going-away party

Step 5

Look at your schedule for the coming week. For each of the items resulting from Step 4, make room on your next week's schedule to take specific action toward accomplishing those goals you have chosen. Write down the goal, the action you will take, and a specific day and time to do it. Consider eliminating plans that are currently on your calendar to find time for your new action items. Duplicate goals may be combined into one action item.

Goal	Action	Day/Time
1. Write a book	Start writing	8–10a.m. Mon.
2. Make museum a catalyst	Develop new leadership on the museum's board	Set up nominating committee
3. Spend summers in Chautauqua	Book house for next summer	Call real estate agent Tues. a.m.
4. Transition to a new career		
5. Secure endowment for museum	Pick chair for endowment campaign	Set up conference call for Fri.
6. Set up financial trusts	Call and set up meeting with lawyer	Meet lawyer before end of month
7. Have a going-away party		

Step 6

Be realistic. Are you struggling to think of an action you can take? Are there items on your list to which you do not want to devote about an hour in the coming week?

In you answer yes to either question, strike that item from your list completely.

Goal	Action	Day/Time
1. Write a book	Start writing	8–10a.m. Mon.
2. Make museum a catalyst	Develop new leadership on the museum's board	Set up nominating committee
3. Spend summers in Chautauqua	Book house for next summer	Call real estate agent Tues. a.m.
~~4. Transition to a new career~~		
5. Secure endowment for museum	Pick chair for endowment campaign	Set up conference call for Fri.
6. Set up financial trusts	Call and set up meeting with lawyer	Meet lawyer before end of month
~~7. Have a going-away party~~		

Step 7

Now you have your final list of most important items. Study it. Search it for broader themes. What do these items say about who you really are and what you want? How do they fit together?

Now, complete the following sentence:

What I want next is:

To be a financially successful writer who improves women lives.

Now, do your own Process.

Remember not to over-think it.

Just write down what first comes to mind.

There are ten extra copies of the Process included in this book so you can do it again whenever you want.

Your answers don't last all your life, nor can you change every aspect of your life at once. Expect your goals to evolve.

Do the Process again and again. Do it when you were expecting a curve ball and you get a slider.

Do it when the kids are grown and the dog is dead.

Do it when you learn something new, get a degree, or dream a dream you cannot forget.

If you have a question, email us at www.whatiwantnext.com.

We will be glad to help you.

Step 1

Spend three minutes listing items to answer this question:

"By the end of my life, what do I want to have done?"

There are no limits...no boundaries...the list should include whatever comes to mind...personal or professional...as large or small as you imagine.

Step 2

Spend three minutes listing items to answer this question:

"By one year from today, what do
I want to have done?"

A year from now is: _________________ (date)

Step 3

Spend three minutes listing items to answer this question:

"I just found out I have thirty days to live.
What do I want to have done in these thirty days?"

Step 4

Look back at each of the first three steps. Circle the three items on each step that are most important to you.
Then, copy them into the grid.

Note: Items may appear more than once in this grid.

Step 1	Step 2	Step 3

Step 5

Look at your schedule for the coming week. For each of the items resulting from Step 4, make room on your next week's schedule to take specific action toward accomplishing those goals you have chosen. Write down the goal, the action you will take, and a specific day and time to do it. Consider eliminating plans that are currently on your calendar to find time for your new action items. Duplicated goals may be combined into one action item.

Goal	Action	Day/Time
1.		
2.		
3.		
4.		
5.		
6.		
7.		
8.		
9.		

Step 6

Be realistic. Are you struggling to think of an action you can take? Are there items on your list to which you do not want to devote about an hour in the coming week?

If you answer yes to either question, go back to Step 5 and strike that item from your list completely.

Step 7

Now you have your final list of most important items. Study it. Search it for broader themes. What do these items say about who you really are and what you want? How do they fit together?

Now, complete the following sentence:

What I want next is:

Epilogue

I like to spend my summers at the Chautauqua Institution in western New York. It is an historic village of Victorian homes on the banks of Chautauqua Lake. For nine weeks every summer, this unique community comes alive with speakers, ballet, symphony music, theatre, visual arts, and lifelong learning classes. It's like a Disneyland for smart adults.

Here you can learn to conduct Mozart or pick up a paintbrush for the first time. To me, learning is what makes life worth living. Learning enables us to change. New brain cells feel good.

"I learn only to be contented." –Japanese Proverb

I finished writing this book beside the lake in Chautauqua. It was the perfect setting—straight out of a movie set. Now that I am a writer, I think I will do the Process again and find out what is next for me.

"That is what learning is. You suddenly understand something you've understood all your life, but in a new way."—Doris Lessing

---

Extra Copies of the ***What I Want Next*** Process for Later Use.

Step 1

Spend three minutes listing items to answer this question:

"By the end of my life, what do I want to have done?"

There are no limits...no boundaries...the list should include whatever comes to mind...personal or professional...as large or small as you imagine.

Step 2

Spend three minutes listing items to answer this question:

"By one year from today, what do
I want to have done?"

A year from now is: _______________ (date)

Step 3

Spend three minutes listing items to answer this question:

"I just found out I have thirty days to live.
What do I want to have done in these thirty days?"

Step 4

Look back at each of the first three steps. Circle the three items on each step that are most important to you.
Then, copy them into the grid.

Note: Items may appear more than once in this grid.

Step 1	Step 2	Step 3

Step 5

Look at your schedule for the coming week. For each of the items resulting from Step 4, make room on your next week's schedule to take specific action toward accomplishing those goals you have chosen. Write down the goal, the action you will take, and a specific day and time to do it. Consider eliminating plans that are currently on your calendar to find time for your new action items. Duplicated goals may be combined into one action item.

Goal	Action	Day/Time
1.		
2.		
3.		
4.		
5.		
6.		
7.		
8.		
9.		

Step 6

Be realistic. Are you struggling to think of an action you can take? Are there items on your list to which you do not want to devote about an hour in the coming week?

If you answer yes to either question, go back to Step 5 and strike that item from your list completely.

Step 7

Now you have your final list of most important items. Study it. Search it for broader themes. What do these items say about who you really are and what you want? How do they fit together?

Now, complete the following sentence:

What I want next is:

Step 1

Spend three minutes listing items to answer this question:

"By the end of my life, what do I want to have done?"

There are no limits...no boundaries...the list should include whatever comes to mind...personal or professional...as large or small as you imagine.

Step 2

Spend three minutes listing items to answer this question:

"By one year from today, what do
I want to have done?"

A year from now is: ________________ (date)

Step 3

Spend three minutes listing items to answer this question:

"I just found out I have thirty days to live.
What do I want to have done in these thirty days?"

Step 4

Look back at each of the first three steps. Circle the three items on each step that are most important to you.
Then, copy them into the grid.

Note: Items may appear more than once in this grid.

Step 1	Step 2	Step 3

Step 5

Look at your schedule for the coming week. For each of the items resulting from Step 4, make room on your next week's schedule to take specific action toward accomplishing those goals you have chosen. Write down the goal, the action you will take, and a specific day and time to do it. Consider eliminating plans that are currently on your calendar to find time for your new action items. Duplicated goals may be combined into one action item.

Goal	Action	Day/Time
1.		
2.		
3.		
4.		
5.		
6.		
7.		
8.		
9.		

Step 6

Be realistic. Are you struggling to think of an action you can take? Are there items on your list to which you do not want to devote about an hour in the coming week?

If you answer yes to either question, go back to Step 5 and strike that item from your list completely.

Step 7

Now you have your final list of most important items. Study it. Search it for broader themes. What do these items say about who you really are and what you want? How do they fit together?

Now, complete the following sentence:

What I want next is:

Step 1

Spend three minutes listing items to answer this question:

"By the end of my life, what do I want to have done?"

There are no limits...no boundaries...the list should include whatever comes to mind...personal or professional...as large or small as you imagine.

Step 2

Spend three minutes listing items to answer this question:

"By one year from today, what do
I want to have done?"

A year from now is: ________________ (date)

Step 3

Spend three minutes listing items to answer this question:

"I just found out I have thirty days to live.
What do I want to have done in these thirty days?"

Step 4

Look back at each of the first three steps. Circle the three items on each step that are most important to you.
Then, copy them into the grid.

Note: Items may appear more than once in this grid.

Step 1	Step 2	Step 3

Step 5

Look at your schedule for the coming week. For each of the items resulting from Step 4, make room on your next week's schedule to take specific action toward accomplishing those goals you have chosen. Write down the goal, the action you will take, and a specific day and time to do it. Consider eliminating plans that are currently on your calendar to find time for your new action items. Duplicated goals may be combined into one action item.

Goal	Action	Day/Time
1.		
2.		
3.		
4.		
5.		
6.		
7.		
8.		
9.		

Step 6

Be realistic. Are you struggling to think of an action you can take? Are there items on your list to which you do not want to devote about an hour in the coming week?

If you answer yes to either question, go back to Step 5 and strike that item from your list completely.

Step 7

Now you have your final list of most important items. Study it. Search it for broader themes. What do these items say about who you really are and what you want? How do they fit together?

Now, complete the following sentence:

What I want next is:

Step 1

Spend three minutes listing items to answer this question:

"By the end of my life, what do I want to have done?"

There are no limits...no boundaries...the list should include whatever comes to mind...personal or professional...as large or small as you imagine.

Step 2

Spend three minutes listing items to answer this question:

"By one year from today, what do I want to have done?"

A year from now is: ________________ (date)

Step 3

Spend three minutes listing items to answer this question:

"I just found out I have thirty days to live.
What do I want to have done in these thirty days?"

Step 4

Look back at each of the first three steps. Circle the three items on each step that are most important to you.
Then, copy them into the grid.

Note: Items may appear more than once in this grid.

Step 1	Step 2	Step 3

Step 5

Look at your schedule for the coming week. For each of the items resulting from Step 4, make room on your next week's schedule to take specific action toward accomplishing those goals you have chosen. Write down the goal, the action you will take, and a specific day and time to do it. Consider eliminating plans that are currently on your calendar to find time for your new action items. Duplicated goals may be combined into one action item.

Goal	Action	Day/Time
1.		
2.		
3.		
4.		
5.		
6.		
7.		
8.		
9.		

Step 6

Be realistic. Are you struggling to think of an action you can take? Are there items on your list to which you do not want to devote about an hour in the coming week?

If you answer yes to either question, go back to Step 5 and strike that item from your list completely.

Step 7

Now you have your final list of most important items. Study it. Search it for broader themes. What do these items say about who you really are and what you want? How do they fit together?

Now, complete the following sentence:

What I want next is:

Step 1

Spend three minutes listing items to answer this question:

"By the end of my life, what do I want to have done?"

There are no limits...no boundaries...the list should include whatever comes to mind...personal or professional...as large or small as you imagine.

Step 2

Spend three minutes listing items to answer this question:

"By one year from today, what do
I want to have done?"

A year from now is: ________________ (date)

Step 3

Spend three minutes listing items to answer this question:

"I just found out I have thirty days to live.
What do I want to have done in these thirty days?"

Step 4

Look back at each of the first three steps. Circle the three items on each step that are most important to you.
Then, copy them into the grid.

Note: Items may appear more than once in this grid.

Step 1	Step 2	Step 3

Step 5

Look at your schedule for the coming week. For each of the items resulting from Step 4, make room on your next week's schedule to take specific action toward accomplishing those goals you have chosen. Write down the goal, the action you will take, and a specific day and time to do it. Consider eliminating plans that are currently on your calendar to find time for your new action items. Duplicated goals may be combined into one action item.

Goal	Action	Day/Time
1.		
2.		
3.		
4.		
5.		
6.		
7.		
8.		
9.		

Step 6

Be realistic. Are you struggling to think of an action you can take? Are there items on your list to which you do not want to devote about an hour in the coming week?

If you answer yes to either question, go back to Step 5 and strike that item from your list completely.

Step 7

Now you have your final list of most important items. Study it. Search it for broader themes. What do these items say about who you really are and what you want? How do they fit together?

Now, complete the following sentence:

What I want next is:

Step 1

Spend three minutes listing items to answer this question:

"By the end of my life, what do I want to have done?"

There are no limits…no boundaries…the list should include whatever comes to mind…personal or professional…as large or small as you imagine.

Step 2

Spend three minutes listing items to answer this question:

"By one year from today, what do
I want to have done?"

A year from now is: _______________ (date)

Step 3

Spend three minutes listing items to answer this question:

"I just found out I have thirty days to live.
What do I want to have done in these thirty days?"

Step 4

Look back at each of the first three steps. Circle the three items on each step that are most important to you.
Then, copy them into the grid.

Note: Items may appear more than once in this grid.

Step 1	Step 2	Step 3

Step 5

Look at your schedule for the coming week. For each of the items resulting from Step 4, make room on your next week's schedule to take specific action toward accomplishing those goals you have chosen. Write down the goal, the action you will take, and a specific day and time to do it. Consider eliminating plans that are currently on your calendar to find time for your new action items. Duplicated goals may be combined into one action item.

Goal	Action	Day/Time
1.		
2.		
3.		
4.		
5.		
6.		
7.		
8.		
9.		

Step 6

Be realistic. Are you struggling to think of an action you can take? Are there items on your list to which you do not want to devote about an hour in the coming week?

If you answer yes to either question, go back to Step 5 and strike that item from your list completely.

Step 7

Now you have your final list of most important items. Study it. Search it for broader themes. What do these items say about who you really are and what you want? How do they fit together?

Now, complete the following sentence:

What I want next is:

Step 1

Spend three minutes listing items to answer this question:

"By the end of my life, what do I want to have done?"

There are no limits...no boundaries...the list should include whatever comes to mind...personal or professional...as large or small as you imagine.

Step 2

Spend three minutes listing items to answer this question:

"By one year from today, what do
I want to have done?"

A year from now is: ________________ (date)

Step 3

Spend three minutes listing items to answer this question:

"I just found out I have thirty days to live.
What do I want to have done in these thirty days?"

Step 4

Look back at each of the first three steps. Circle the three items on each step that are most important to you.
Then, copy them into the grid.

Note: Items may appear more than once in this grid.

Step 1	Step 2	Step 3

Step 5

Look at your schedule for the coming week. For each of the items resulting from Step 4, make room on your next week's schedule to take specific action toward accomplishing those goals you have chosen. Write down the goal, the action you will take, and a specific day and time to do it. Consider eliminating plans that are currently on your calendar to find time for your new action items. Duplicated goals may be combined into one action item.

Goal	Action	Day/Time
1.		
2.		
3.		
4.		
5.		
6.		
7.		
8.		
9.		

Step 6

Be realistic. Are you struggling to think of an action you can take? Are there items on your list to which you do not want to devote about an hour in the coming week?

If you answer yes to either question, go back to Step 5 and strike that item from your list completely.

Step 7

Now you have your final list of most important items. Study it. Search it for broader themes. What do these items say about who you really are and what you want? How do they fit together?

Now, complete the following sentence:

What I want next is:

Step 1

Spend three minutes listing items to answer this question:

"By the end of my life, what do I want to have done?"

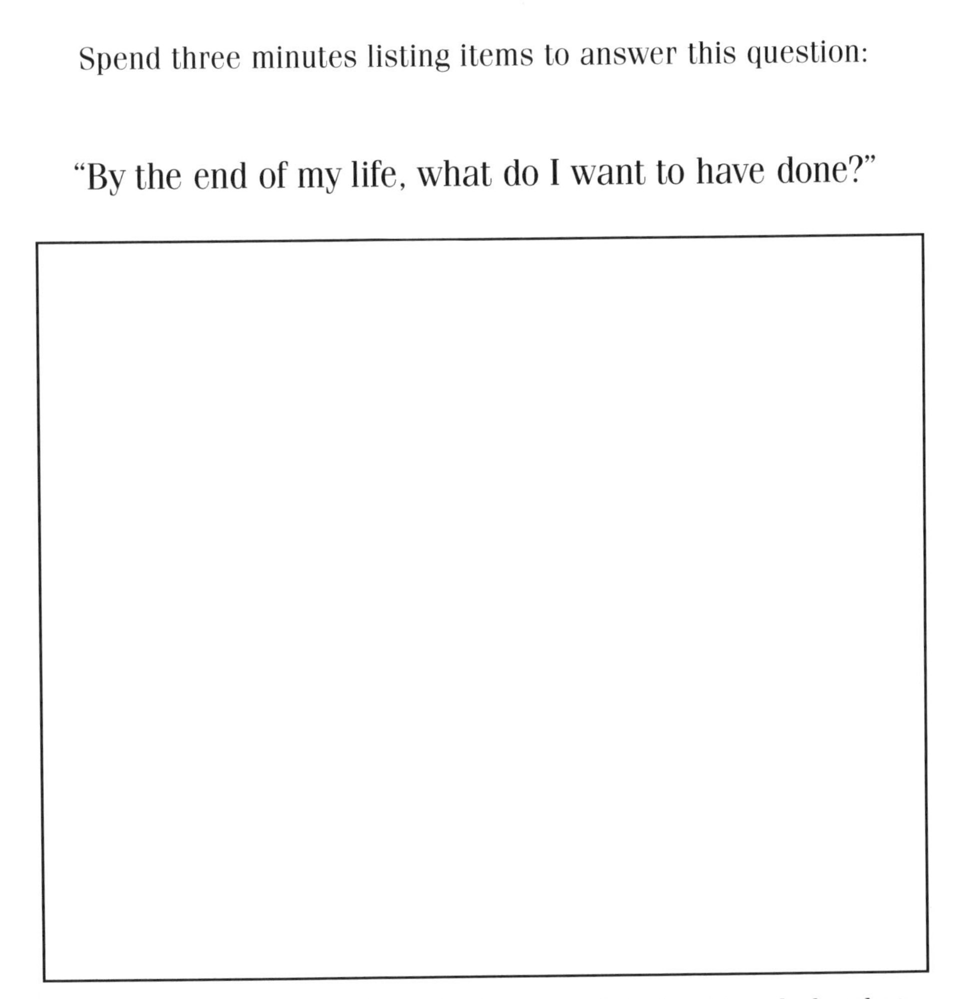

There are no limits...no boundaries...the list should include whatever comes to mind...personal or professional...as large or small as you imagine.

Step 2

Spend three minutes listing items to answer this question:

"By one year from today, what do
I want to have done?"

A year from now is: ________________ (date)

Step 3

Spend three minutes listing items to answer this question:

"I just found out I have thirty days to live.
What do I want to have done in these thirty days?"

Step 4

Look back at each of the first three steps. Circle the three items on each step that are most important to you.
Then, copy them into the grid.

Note: Items may appear more than once in this grid.

Step 1	Step 2	Step 3

Step 5

Look at your schedule for the coming week. For each of the items resulting from Step 4, make room on your next week's schedule to take specific action toward accomplishing those goals you have chosen. Write down the goal, the action you will take, and a specific day and time to do it. Consider eliminating plans that are currently on your calendar to find time for your new action items. Duplicated goals may be combined into one action item.

Goal	Action	Day/Time
1.		
2.		
3.		
4.		
5.		
6.		
7.		
8.		
9.		

Step 6

Be realistic. Are you struggling to think of an action you can take? Are there items on your list to which you do not want to devote about an hour in the coming week?

If you answer yes to either question, go back to Step 5 and strike that item from your list completely.

Step 7

Now you have your final list of most important items. Study it. Search it for broader themes. What do these items say about who you really are and what you want? How do they fit together?

Now, complete the following sentence:

What I want next is:

Step 1

Spend three minutes listing items to answer this question:

"By the end of my life, what do I want to have done?"

There are no limits...no boundaries...the list should include whatever comes to mind...personal or professional...as large or small as you imagine.

Step 2

Spend three minutes listing items to answer this question:

"By one year from today, what do
I want to have done?"

A year from now is: ________________ (date)

Step 3

Spend three minutes listing items to answer this question:

"I just found out I have thirty days to live.
What do I want to have done in these thirty days?"

Step 4

Look back at each of the first three steps. Circle the three items on each step that are most important to you.
Then, copy them into the grid.

Note: Items may appear more than once in this grid.

Step 1	Step 2	Step 3

Step 5

Look at your schedule for the coming week. For each of the items resulting from Step 4, make room on your next week's schedule to take specific action toward accomplishing those goals you have chosen. Write down the goal, the action you will take, and a specific day and time to do it. Consider eliminating plans that are currently on your calendar to find time for your new action items. Duplicated goals may be combined into one action item.

Goal	Action	Day/Time
1.		
2.		
3.		
4.		
5.		
6.		
7.		
8.		
9.		

Step 6

Be realistic. Are you struggling to think of an action you can take? Are there items on your list to which you do not want to devote about an hour in the coming week?

If you answer yes to either question, go back to Step 5 and strike that item from your list completely.

Step 7

Now you have your final list of most important items. Study it. Search it for broader themes. What do these items say about who you really are and what you want? How do they fit together?

Now, complete the following sentence:

What I want next is:

Step 1

Spend three minutes listing items to answer this question:

"By the end of my life, what do I want to have done?"

There are no limits...no boundaries...the list should include whatever comes to mind...personal or professional...as large or small as you imagine.

Step 2

Spend three minutes listing items to answer this question:

"By one year from today, what do
I want to have done?"

A year from now is: ________________ (date)

Step 3

Spend three minutes listing items to answer this question:

"I just found out I have thirty days to live.
What do I want to have done in these thirty days?"

Step 4

Look back at each of the first three steps. Circle the three items on each step that are most important to you.
Then, copy them into the grid.

Note: Items may appear more than once in this grid.

Step 1	Step 2	Step 3

Step 5

Look at your schedule for the coming week. For each of the items resulting from Step 4, make room on your next week's schedule to take specific action toward accomplishing those goals you have chosen. Write down the goal, the action you will take, and a specific day and time to do it. Consider eliminating plans that are currently on your calendar to find time for your new action items. Duplicated goals may be combined into one action item.

Goal	Action	Day/Time
1.		
2.		
3.		
4.		
5.		
6.		
7.		
8.		
9.		

Step 6

Be realistic. Are you struggling to think of an action you can take? Are there items on your list to which you do not want to devote about an hour in the coming week?

If you answer yes to either question, go back to Step 5 and strike that item from your list completely.

Step 7

Now you have your final list of most important items. Study it. Search it for broader themes. What do these items say about who you really are and what you want? How do they fit together?

Now, complete the following sentence:

What I want next is:

What I Want Next

books to come:

What I Want Next for My Health

What I Want Next for My Relationship

What I Want Next for My Parents

What I Want Next While I Work at Home

What I Want Next in a President

What I Want Next for My Retirement

What I Want Next for My Education

Made in the USA
Middletown, DE
24 September 2024

61386147R00092